25
PROPHETS
OF
ISLAM

Irfan Alli

REVIEWS: I would appreciate reading your thoughts after you have read this book. To make this possible please go to www.amazon.com search the title of the book and post a review. Thanks for taking the time!

CONTACT: Irfan Alli can be reached at irfanalli@irfanalli.com

25 PROPHETS OF ISLAM

Ever wondered who is a prophet, and if there is a connection between the work of one prophet and another? This book explains the role of a prophet and the relationship between the work of one prophet and another while sharing with you the names and lives of some of the prophets of Islam.

The prophets of Islam include: Adam, Idris (Enoch), Nuh (Noah), Hud (Heber), Saleh (Methusaleh), Lut (Lot), Ibrahim (Abraham), Ismail (Ishmael), Ishaq (Isaac), Yaqub (Jacob), Yusuf (Joseph), Shu'aib (Jethro), Ayyub (Job), Dhulkifl (Ezekiel), Musa (Moses), Harun (Aaron), Dawud (David), Sulayman (Solomon), Ilyas (Elias), Alyasa (Elisha), Yunus (Jonah), Zakariya (Zachariah), Yahya (John the Baptist), Isa (Jesus) and Muhammad. Peace be upon them all.

In *25 Prophets of Islam* you will learn:

moses – 10 commandments

1. That God is one.
2. About revelations mentioned in the Quran.
3. That the prophets were Muslims.
4. That Jesus was not the son of God.
5. Who committed the first murder.
6. About the similarity between Adam and Jesus.
7. What the Quran says about homosexuality.
8. Which prophet God spoke to direct.
9. That Jesus was not crucified and will come again.

Find out about these and other issues by reading this book.

Prophets – individuals who recived direct message from God, some are massengers
Apostels by christians spreding the massage of Prophets

3

Irfan Alli is an author, motivational speaker, enlightenment instigator and futurist. His volunteer efforts, professional work and recreational activities have taken him all across Canada, to the U.S., Brazil, Hong Kong, Indonesia, South Korea, Japan, Guyana, Pakistan, India, Jordan, Saudi Arabia, China, Turkey, Portugal and Spain. What he has learned from his travels is reflected in his books and speeches. Irfan lives in Toronto, Canada with his wife, four children and ten grand children.

Some of his book titles are:

1. 101 Selected Sayings of Buddha

2. What are Angels?

3. 101 Selected Sayings of Prophet Muhammad (peace be upon him)

4. Family Makeovers

5. 101 Selected Sayings of Mahatma Gandhi

6. Enlightenment from the Quran – God's Last Revelation to Mankind

7. 25 Prophets of Islam

8. 201 Motivational Quotes from Around the World

9. Spouse Trap – Over 200 Questions to Ask Before Saying 'I do'

To find out more visit www.irfanalli.com

TABLE OF CONTENTS

INTRODUCTION

Questions like: What is the purpose of life? How should life be lived? Who is God? What should one look for in a spouse? How should one raise one's children? What happens after death? What are angels? Who are prophets and what are their roles? are all addressed in the Quran and Hadith (the sayings and practices of prophet Muhammad, peace be upon him), the two sources of Islam's teachings.

Muslims believe that the same angel Gabriel that came to prophets Abraham, Moses and Jesus also came to Muhammad (peace be upon them all). Muslims also believe that God, through the angel Gabriel, revealed the Quran to Muhammad (peace be upon him). This was done over a period of twenty-three years. Muslims consider the Quran to be God's last revelation to mankind. Since one in every five persons on earth is a Muslim, the Quran enlightens and guides over one billion people around the world.

The Hadith are the sayings and practices of prophet Muhammad (peace be upon him). Muhammad (peace be upon him) lived during the sixth and seventh centuries. Muslims accept him as God's last prophet and messenger to mankind. He invited people to the same God that Abraham, Moses and Jesus (peace be upon them) invited people to. The sayings of prophet Muhammad (peace be upon him) number in the thousands and cover a variety of topics.

This book will look at what these two sources say regarding prophets and list the 25 prophets mentioned in the Quran.

Irfan Alli.

AN ARTICLE OF FAITH

The faith of a Muslim (a follower of Islam) consists of various beliefs. It includes the belief in:

1. God
2. His Books
3. **His Prophets**
4. His Angels
5. The Last Day

This book focuses on the belief in prophets. We will discuss who they are, their responsibilities, how they relate to our lives, and the connections between the teachings of all of God's prophets.

The Quran teaches:

"O you who believe! Believe in God and His Messenger, and the scripture which He has sent to His Messenger and the scripture which He sent to those before (him). Any who denies God, His angels, His Books, **His Messengers**, and the Day of Judgement, has gone far, far astray." (Quran 4:136)

"It is not righteousness that you turn your faces towards east or west; but it is righteousness - to believe in God and the Last Day. And the angels, and the Books, **and the Messengers**; to spend of your substance, out of love for Him, for your kin, for orphans, for the needy, for the wayfarer. For those who ask, and for the ransom of slaves; to be steadfast in prayer, and give Zakah (charity), to fulfill the contracts which you have made; and to be firm and patient, in pain (or suffering) and adversity, and throughout all periods of panic. Such are the people of truth, the God-fearing." (Quran 2:177)

As you can see from the above verse it is part of righteousness for a Muslim to believe in all of God's messengers.

THE ROLE OF PROPHETS

Muslims believe that Adam (peace be upon him) was the first prophet and Muhammad (peace be upon him) was the last prophet, and in between the two of them there were numerous prophets sent. The prophets were all human beings inspired and supported by God. God instructs us:

"Say: 'We believe in God, and in what has been revealed to us and what was revealed to Abraham, Ishmael, Isaac, Jacob, and the Tribes, and in (the Books) given to Moses, Jesus, and the Prophets, from their Lord: we make no distinction between one and another among them, and to God we bow our will (in Islam).' " (Quran 3:84)

"We have sent you inspiration, as We sent it to Noah and the Messengers after him: We sent inspiration to Abraham, Ishmael, Issac, Jacob and the Tribes, to Jesus, Job, Jonah, Aaron, and Solomon, and to David We gave the Psalms." Quran 4:163)

Belief in all the prophets of God is essential in Islam because all of the prophets were sent by the same one God. To accept some and reject others could imply a racial bias or ignorance about the role of prophets. All prophets invited people to the same God and conveyed whatever guidance they were asked to share with mankind at that stage in mankind's spiritual evolution and history.

Islam teaches that God created man with a purpose. From the beginning of man's existence God sent prophets to different nations to remind man of this purpose. They each reminded man to worship God alone and abandon all false deities. God says in the Quran:

"For We assuredly sent amongst every People a Messenger, (with the command): "Serve God, and eschew Evil;" of the people were some whom God guided, and some on whom Error became inevitably (established). So travel through the earth, and see what was the end of those who denied (the Truth)." (Quran 16:36)

REVELATIONS FROM GOD

To some of the prophets God sent revelations through the angel Gabriel. As human society evolved, the content of the revelation evolved with it. The Quran tells us:

a) The Scrolls were given to Abraham (peace be upon him):

"And this is in the Books of the earliest (Revelations), The Books of Abraham and Moses." (Quran 87:18-19)

b) The Psalms were given to David (peace be upon him):

"And it is your Lord that knows best all beings that are in the heavens and on earth: and We made some of the Prophets to excel others and We gave to David the Psalms." (Quran 17:55)

"We have sent you inspiration, as We sent it to Noah and the Messengers after him: We sent inspiration to Abraham, Ishmael, Issac, Jacob and the Tribes, to Jesus, Job, Jonah, Aaron, and Solomon, and to David We gave the Psalms." (Quran 4:163)

c) The Old Testament was given to Moses (peace be upon him):

"No just estimate of God do they make when they say: 'Nothing does God send down to man (by way of revelation)': Say: 'Who then sent down the Book which Moses brought?- a light and guidance to man: but you make it into (separate) sheets for show, while you conceal much (of its contents): therein were you taught that which you knew not -neither you nor your fathers.' Say: 'God (sent it down)': then leave them to plunge in vain discourse and trifling." (Quran 6:91)

d) The New Testament was given to Jesus (peace be upon him):

"And in their footsteps We sent Jesus the son of Mary, confirming the Torah that had come before him: We sent him the Gospel: therein was guidance and light. And confirmation of the Torah that had come before him: a guidance and an admonition to those who fear God." (Quran 5:46)

e) The Quran was given to Muhammad (peace be upon him):

"It is He who sent down to you (step by step), in truth, the Quran, confirming what went before it; and He sent down the Torah (of Moses) and the Gospel (of Jesus). Before this, as a guide to mankind, and He sent down the Criterion (of judgement between right and wrong). Then those who reject faith in the Signs of God will suffer the severest chastisement and God is Exalted in might, Lord of retribution." (Quran 3:3-4)

As we mentioned earlier belief in the revelations of God is one of the articles of faith for Muslims. However, since we are missing the original texts of the earlier revelations, Muslims only follow those parts of the earlier revelation that is in harmony with the Quran. As for keeping the Quran from being tampered with, it has always been with the people in both a written and memorized format, preventing any kinds of tampering or changes. Further, God says:

"We have, without doubt, sent down the Quran; and We will assuredly guard it (from corruption)." (Quran 15:9)

HOW MANY PROPHETS WERE SENT?

By now, you may be wondering how many prophets God sent to mankind. Nobody knows for sure. What we know is what God has told us in the Quran.

God says he sent a prophet to every nation. He says:

"For We assuredly sent amongst every People a Messenger, (with the command): 'Serve God, and eschew Evil;' of the people were some whom God guided, and some on whom Error became inevitably (established). So travel through the earth, and see what was the end of those who denied (the Truth)" (Quran 16:36)

This is because one of the principles by which God operates is that He will never take a people to task unless He has made clear to them what His expectations are.

God mentions in the Quran the names of 25 prophets and indicates there were others. God says:

"Of some messengers We have already told you the story; of others We have not; - and to Moses God spoke direct." (Quran 4:164)

Later in this book we will sample portions of the Quran that speaks about the lives of some prophets. Let us first find out the names of the twenty-five mentioned in the Quran.

25 PROPHETS MENTIONED IN THE QURAN

The names of the twenty-five prophets mentioned are as follows:
Adam
Idris (Enoch)
Nuh (Noah)
Hud (Heber)
Saleh (Methusaleh)
Lut (Lot)
Ibrahim (Abraham)
Ismail (Ishmael)
Ishaq (Isaac)
Yaqub (Jacob)
Yusuf (Joseph)
Shu'aib (Jethro)
Ayyub (Job)
Dhulkifl (Ezekiel)
Musa (Moses)
Harun (Aaron)
Dawud (David)
Sulaiman (Solomon)
Ilyas (Elias)
Alyasa (Elisha)
Yunus (Jonah)
Zakariya (Zachariah)
Yahya (John the Baptist)
Isa (Jesus)
Muhammad

Peace be upon them all.

WORSHIP ONE GOD

The main message the various prophets of God brought to mankind, despite the people they were sent to and the time in history they appeared, was that God is one and to worship Him alone. Below is a sampling of what God revealed in the Quran.

NOAH/NUH
(peace be upon him)
And indeed We sent Noah to his people, and he said: "O my people! Worship God! You have no other God but Him. Will you not then be afraid of Him (i.e. of His Punishment because of worshipping others besides Him)?" (Quran 23:23)

HEBER/HUD
(peace be upon him)
And to 'Aad [We sent] their brother Heber. He said, "O my people, worship God; you have no deity other than Him. You are not but inventors [of falsehood]. (Quran 11:50)

METHUSALEH/SALEH
(peace be upon him)
And to Thamud [We sent] their brother Methusaleh. He said, "O my people, worship God; you have no deity other than Him. He has produced you from the earth and settled you in it, so ask forgiveness of Him and then repent to Him. Indeed, my Lord is near and responsive." (Quran 11:61)

ABRAHAM/IBRAHIM
(peace be upon him)
And (remember) Abraham when he said to his people: "Worship God (alone), and fear Him, that is better for you if you did but know. (Quran 29:16)

JETHRO/SHU'AIB
(peace be upon him)
And to Madyan [We sent] their brother Jethro. He said, "O my people, worship God; you have no deity other than Him. And do not decrease from the measure and the scale. Indeed, I see you in prosperity, but indeed, I fear for you the punishment of an all-encompassing Day. (Quran 11:84)

1015

MUHAMMAD
(peace be upon him)

Say, [O Muhammad], "I am only a warner, and there is not any deity except God , the One, the Prevailing. (Quran 38:65)

God summarizes all of this in another verse when he says:

"For We assuredly sent amongst every People a Messenger, (with the command): "Serve God, and eschew Evil;" of the people were some whom God guided, and some on whom Error became inevitably (established). So travel through the earth, and see what was the end of those who denied (the Truth)." (Quran 16:36)

THE PROPHETS AND THEIR FOLLOWERS WERE MUSLIMS

Since all prophets invited to the same one God, Muslims see them as all inviting to the same religion as well, the religion of Islam. **Islam** is an attributive title. It literally means peace, submission, and obedience. In the religious sense, Islam means: The way to peace and salvation through submission to the will of God and by obedience to His laws.

A person who chooses this path is called a **Muslim**. The Quran therefore describes the prophets and their followers as Muslims.

In the Quran Abraham, Moses, and Jesus (peace be upon them) are mentioned as praying to God to make them **Muslims,** or instructing their people to be **Muslims**. That is, one who submits to God.

Here is what God reveals in the Quran on:

ABRAHAM (peace be upon him)
Abraham (peace be upon him) prayed:
"Our Lord! Make of us **Muslims**, bowing to Your (Will), and of our progeny a people **Muslim**, bowing to Your (Will); and show us our places for the celebration of (due) rites; and turn to us (in mercy); for you are the Oft-Relenting, Most Merciful." (Quran 2:128)

MOSES (peace be upon him)
"Moses said: 'O my People! If you do (really) believe in God, then in Him put your trust if you are **Muslims**.'" (Quran 10:84)

JESUS (peace be upon him)
"And behold! I inspired the Disciples to have faith in Me and My Messenger; they said: 'We have faith, and do bear witness that we bow to God as **Muslims**." (Quran 5:11)

Prophet Muhammad (peace be upon him) said:

"Both in this world and in the Hereafter, I am the nearest of all people to Jesus, the son of Mary. The prophets are paternal brothers; their mothers are different, but their religion is one." (Abu Huraira in Bukhari, Volume 4, pg. 434, # 652)

Islam therefore is not a new religion, but the way of life taught by all the prophets of God. Amongst them - Abraham, Moses, Jesus and Muhammad (peace be upon them).

On accepting and living Islam one therefore accepts all the prophets of the past, recognizing that God's religion is one and historically connected. All prophets got their guidance from the same God, and each invited to the same way of life - **Islam.**

Here are some selected verses from the Quran on some of the twenty-five prophets mentioned in the Quran. Should you be further interested, you can then read the rest of the Quran on your own to get each of their full stories.

ADAM
(peace be upon him)

There are a lot of similarities between the Bible and the Quran on Prophet Adam (peace be upon him). There are similarities because the angel that brought revelation to Prophet Jesus (peace be upon him) was the same angel, angel Gabriel, that brought revelation to Prophet Muhammad (peace be upon them). Here are some excerpts from the Quran on Prophet Adam (peace be upon him):

ADAM CREATED FROM CLAY
"He created man (Adam) from sounding clay like the clay of pottery." (Quran 55:14).

SIMILARITY BETWEEN ADAM AND JESUS
"Verily the likeness of Jesus, in God's Sight is the likeness of Adam, He created him from the dust then He said to him "Be!" --and he (Jesus) was. (Quran 3:59).

From the above verse, it would make more sense, that if one wanted to worship a man they should worship Adam not Jesus, as Adam had no earthly father or mother, while Jesus had a mother but no father (peace be on both of them). Adam's creation is more miraculous!

ONCE LIVED IN PARADISE
"O Adam! Dwell you and your wife in Paradise and eat both of you freely with pleasure and delight of things therein as wherever you will, but come not near this tree or you both will be of the wrong doers."(Quran 2:35)

SATAN MISLED ADAM AND EVE AND THEY WERE SENT TO EARTH
"Then Satan whispered suggestions to them both in order to uncover that which was hidden from them of their private parts before, he said:" Your Lord did not forbid you this tree save you should become angels or become of the immortals." Satan swore by God to them both saying: "Verily I am one of the sincere well wishers for you both." So he misled them with deception. Then when they tasted of the tree, that which was hidden from them of their shame (private parts) became manifest to them and they began to stick together the leaves of Paradise over themselves (in order to cover their shame). Their Lord called out to them saying "Did I not forbid you that tree and tell you, Verily Satan is an open enemy unto you?" They said: "Our Lord! We have wronged ourselves. If You forgive us not, and bestow not upon us Your Mercy, we shall certainly be of the losers." God said: "Get down one of you an enemy to the other (i.e. Adam, Eve, and Satan etc). On earth will be a dwelling place for you and an enjoyment, for a time." He said:

"therein you shall live, and therein you shall die, and from it you shall be brought out (resurrected)." (Quran 7:11-25).

WE ARE ALL DECENDANTS OF ADAM AND EVE

"O Mankind! Be dutiful to your Lord, Who created you from a single person (Adam) and from Him (Adam) He created his wife (Eve), and from them both He created many men and women. (Quran 4:1)

LET NOT SATAN DECEIVE YOU, AS HE DECEIVED ADAM

"O Children of Adam! Let not Satan deceive you, as he got your parents (Adam and Eve) out of Paradise stripping them of their raiment; to show them their private parts. Verily he (Satan) and his soldiers from the jinn or his tribe see you from where you cannot see them. Verily, We made the devils (protectors and helpers) for those who believe not." (Quran 7:27)

THE FIRST MURDER

" And (O Muhammad) recite to them (the Jews) the story of the two sons of Adam (Abel and Cain) in truth; when each offered a sacrifice to God, it was accepted from the one but not from the other. The latter said to the former; "I will surely kill you. "The former said: "Verily God accepts only from those who are pious. If you do stretch your hand against me to kill me I shall never stretch my hand against you to kill you, for I fear God; the Lord of the Worlds (mankind, jinn, and all that exists). Verily I intend to let you draw my sin on yourself as well as yours then you will be one of the dwellers of the Fire, and that is the recompense of the polytheists, and wrongdoers. "So the self of the other (latter one) encouraged him and made fair seeming to him the murder of his brother; he murdered him and became one of the losers. God sent a crow who scratched the ground to show him to hide the dead body of his brother. He (the murderer) said: "Woe to me! Am I not even able to be as this crow and to hide the dead body of my brother?" Then he became one of those who regretted. (Quran 5:27-31).

NOAH/NUH
(peace be upon him)

The people of Noah had deteriorated to the point where they were worshipping statues they called Gods. They gave these statues names like Wadd, Suwa, Yaghuth, Yauq, and Nasr. This lead to Prophet Noah (peace be upon him) trying to get his people to return to worshipping God alone.

NOAH TRIED TO BRING HIS PEOPLE BACK TO GOD
"Indeed We sent Noah to his people (he said): "I have come to you as a plain Warner that you worship none but God, surely, I fear for you the torment of a painful Day." The chiefs of the disbelievers among his people said: "We see you but a man like ourselves, nor do we see any follow you but the meanest among us and they too followed you without thinking. And we do not see in you any merit above us in fact we think you are a liar." (Quran 11:25-27).

And indeed We sent Noah to his people, and he said: "O my people! Worship God! You have no other God but Him. Will you not then be afraid of Him i.e. of His Punishment because of worshipping others besides Him)?" (Quran 23:23)

THEY REFUSED TO GIVE UP THEIR IDOLS
"They (idolaters) have said: "You shall not leave your gods nor shall we leave Wadd, nor Suwa, nor Yaghuth, nor Yauq nor Nasr (names of the idols)." (Quran 71:23).

They then dared Prophet Noah (peace be upon him) to have God punish them for their idol worship. Here is what unfolded:

NOAH'S PEOPLE ASKED FOR HIM TO DELIVER ON HIS THREAT
They said: "O Noah! You have disputed with us and much have you prolonged the dispute with us, now bring upon us what you threaten us with, if you are of the truthful." He said: "Only God will bring it (the punishment) on you, if He will, and then you will escape not. And my advice will not profit you, even if I wish to give you counsel, if God's Will is to keep you astray. He is your Lord! And to Him you shall return." (Quran 11:32-34)

NOAH PRAYS FOR THEIR DISTRUCTION
"My Lord! Leave not one of the disbelievers on the earth. If you leave them, they will mislead Your slaves and they will beget none but wicked disbelievers." (Quran 71:27)

GOD INSTRUCTS NOAH TO BUILD AN ARK

"And construct the ship under Our Eyes and with Our Inspiration and address Me not on behalf of those who did wrong; they are surely to be drowned." (Quran 11:37)

"As he was constructing the ship, whenever the chiefs of his people passed by him, they made a mockery of him. He said : "If you mock at us, so do we mock at you likewise for your mocking. And you will know who it is on whom will come a torment that will cover him with disgrace and on whom will fall a lasting torment." (Quran 11:38-39)

THE FLOOD COMES AND NOAH'S SON DROWNS WITH THE OTHERS

"Embark therein in the Name of God will be its moving course and its resting anchorage. Surely, my Lord is Oft Forgiving, most Merciful." So it (the ship) sailed with them amidst the waves like mountains, and Noah called out to his son, who had separated himself (apart), "O my son! Embark with us and be not with the disbelievers." The son replied, "I will betake myself to a mountain, it will save me from the water." Noah said: "This day there is no savior from the Decree of God except him on whom He has mercy." And a wave came in between them so he (the son) was among the drowned." (Quran 11: 41-43)

THE FLOOD ENDS AND THE ARK COMES TO REST ON MOUNT JUDI

"O Earth! Swallow up your water, and O sky! Withhold (your rain)." The water was diminished (made to subside) and the Decree (of God) was fulfilled (the destruction of the people of Noah). And it (the ship) rested on Mount Judi, and it was said: "Away with the people who are polytheists, and into wrongdoing)!" And it was said: "O Noah! Come down (from the ship) with peace from Us and blessings on you and on the people who are with you (and on some of their offspring), but (there will be other) people to whom We shall grant their pleasures (for a time), but in the end a painful torment will reach them from Us." (Quran 11: 41-48)

ABRAHAM / IBRAHIM
(peace be upon him)

Abraham was chosen by God to be the father of a great religious movement with a universal call. From his offspring came great prophets and an invitation to God.

It is known that Abraham had two sons Isaac and Ishmael. Prophets Moses and Jesus are descendants of Prophet Isaac, and Prophet Muhammad descended from Prophet Ishmael (peace be upon them all).

The Quran is filled with all kinds of interesting stories around Prophet Abraham (peace be upon him). For example:

ABRAHAM'S SEARCH FOR GOD
"Lo! Abraham said to his father Azar: 'Do you take idols for gods? For I see you and your people in manifest error.' So also did We show Abraham the kingdom of the heavens and the earth, that he might have certitude. When the night covered him over, he saw a star, he said: 'This is my Lord.' But when it set, he said, 'I love not those that set.' When he saw the moon rising in splendor, he said: 'This is my Lord.' But when the moon set, he said: 'Unless my Lord guide me, I shall surely be among those who go astray.' When he saw the sun rising (in splendor) he said: 'This is my Lord; this is the greatest (of all).' But when the sun set, he said: 'O my people! I am indeed free from your (guilt) of giving partners to God. For me, I have set my face firmly and truly, towards Him who created the heavens and the earth, and never shall I give partners to God.'" (Quran 6:74-79)

ASKED GOD TO SHOW HIM HOW HE GAVE LIFE TO THE DEAD
Behold! Abraham said: 'My Lord! Show me how you give life to the dead,' He said: 'Do you not then believe?' He said: 'Yea! But to satisfy my own heart.' He said: 'Take four birds, tie them (cut them into pieces), then put a portion of them: on every hill, and call to them: they will come to you (flying) with speed. Then know that God is Exalted in power, Wise.' " (Quran 2: 258-260)

CHALLENGES THE PRACTICES OF HIS PEOPLE
"We bestowed aforetime on Abraham his rectitude of conduct, and well were We acquainted with him. Behold! He said to his father and his people, 'What are these images, to which you are (so assiduously) devoted?' They said, ' We found our fathers worshipping them.' He said, 'Indeed you have been in manifest error- you and your fathers.' The said, 'Have you brought us the Truth, or are you one of those who jest?' He said, 'Nay, your Lord is the Lord of the heavens and the earth, He Who created them (from nothing): and I am a witness to this (truth). And by

God I will certainly plan against your idols, after you go away and turn your backs'... So he broke them to pieces, (all) but the biggest of them, that they might turn (and address themselves) to it. They said, 'Who has done this to our gods? He must indeed be one of the unjust ones. They said, 'We heard a youth talk of them: He is called Abraham.' They said, 'Then bring him before the eyes of the people, that they may bear witness.' They said, 'Are you the one that did this with our gods, O Abraham?' He said: 'Nay, this was done by this the biggest one! Ask them, if they can talk.' So they turned to themselves and said, 'Surely you are the ones in the wrong!' Then were they confounded with shame; (they said), 'you know full well that these (idols) do not speak!' (Abraham) said, 'Do you then worship, besides God, things that can neither be of any good to you nor do you harm? Fie upon you, and upon the things that you worship besides God! Have you no sense?'..." (Quran 21:51-67)

ABRAHAM TRIED TO BRING HIS PEOPLE BACK TO GOD
And (remember) Abraham when he said to his people: "Worship God (alone), and fear Him, that is better for you if you did but know. (Quran 29:16)

HIS PEOPLE TRIED TO BURN HIM, BUT GOD COOLED THE FIRE
"They said, 'Burn him and protect your gods, if you do (anything at all)!' We said, 'O Fire! Be cool, and (a means of) safety for Abraham!' " (Quran 21:68-69)

ARGUED WITH GREAT WISDOM AGAINST THE KING
"Have you not turned your thought to one who disputed with Abraham about his Lord, because God had granted him power? Abraham said: 'My Lord is He Who gives life and death.' He said: 'I give life and death.' Said Abraham: 'But it is God who causes the sun to rise from the east: cause it then to rise from the west.' Thus was he confounded who (in arrogance) rejected faith. Nor does God give guidance to a people unjust." (Quran 2:258)

LOT/LUT
(peace be upon him)

I was fortunate enough to have visited Jordan. Jordan is filled with a lot of religious history. Amongst which is the story of Prophet Lot (peace be upon him) and his people. The Dead Sea, which separates Israel and Jordan, is where Lot's town was turned upside down. Below are some excerpts of the story:

LOT WARNS HIS PEOPLE ABOUT HOMOSEXUALITY
God the Almighty revealed: The people of Lot (who dwelt in the towns of Sodom in Palestine) belied the Messengers when their brother Lot said to them: "Will you not fear God and obey Him? Verily! I am a trustworthy Messenger to you. So fear God, keep your duty to Him, and obey me. No reward do I ask of you for it (my Message of Islamic Monotheism) my reward is only from the Lord of the Worlds. Go you with the males of mankind, and leave those whom God has created for you to be your wives? Nay, you are a trespassing people!" They said: "If you cease not, O Lot! Verily, you will be one of those who are driven out!" He said: "I am indeed, of those who disapprove with severe anger and fury this evil action (of sodomy). My Lord! Save me and my family from what they do." So We saved him and his family, all except his wife, she was among those who remained behind. (Quran 26:160-171)

LOT'S WIFE WAS A DISBELIEVER
You may think a prophet has the power to make people believers. That power is with God only. Some prophets even lost family members to disbelief. Amongst them was the wife of Noah and the wife of Lot.

"God set forth an example for those who disbelieve, the wife of Noah and the wife of Lot. They were under two of Our righteous slaves, but they both betrayed their husbands (by rejecting their doctrines), so they profited nothing before on their account, but were told: "Enter the Fire along with those who enter!" (Quran 66:10)

LOT'S PEOPLE TOLD HIM TO DELIVER ON HIS THREAT
"Bring God's Torment upon us if you are one of the truthful!" (Quran 29:29).

ANGELS WERE SENT TO DESTROY THE TOWN
They (the angels) said: "We have been sent to a people who are disbelievers (polytheists, sinners). (All) except the family of Lot. Them we are surely going to save (from destruction)." Except his wife, of whom We have decreed that she shall be of the those who remain behind (she will be destroyed). Then when the Messengers (the angels) came unto the family of Lot, he said: "Verily! You are

people unknown to me." They said: "Nay! we have come to you with that (torment) which they have been doubting. And we have brought to you the truth (the news of the destruction of your nation) and certainly, we tell the truth. Then travel in a part of the night with your family, and you go behind them in the rear, and let no one amongst you look back, but go on to where you are ordered."

And We made known this decree to him, that the root of those (sinners) was to be cut off in the early morning. The inhabitants of the city came rejoicing (at the news of the young men's arrival). Lot said: "Verily! These are my guests, so shame me not. And fear God and disgrace me not." They (people of the city) said: "Did we not forbid you to entertain (or protect) any of the people (foreigners strangers etc) from us?" Lot said: "These (the girls of the nation) are my daughters to marry lawfully) if you must act so." Verily, by your life (O Muhammad), in their wild intoxication they were wandering blindly. So as torment overtook them at the time of sunrise; and We turned the towns of Sodom (in Palestine) upside down and rained down on them stones of baked clay. Surely! In this are signs for those who see (or understand or learn the lessons from the Signs of God). And verily! They (the cities) are right on the highroad (from Mecca to Syria, i.e. the place where the Dead Sea is now). Surely! Therein is indeed a sign for the believers." (Quran 15:58-77)

LOT AND HIS FAMILY SAVED

"So we saved him and his family, all, except his wife among those who remained behind. Then afterward We destroyed the others. We rained on them a rain of torment. How evil was the reign of those who had been warned. Verily, in this is indeed a sign yet most of them are not believers. Verily! Your Lord, He is indeed the All Mighty, the Most Merciful. (Quran 26:170-175)

JOSEPH/YUSUF
(peace be upon him)

Prophet Joseph (peace be upon him) had to constantly find a way out of plots perpetrated by people close to him. His story is filled with betrayal, slavery, attempted seduction, imprisonment, dream interpretation and the rise to power.
It starts out with his brothers thinking of killing him. Instead he was abandoned by his brothers at a young age. He ended up being sold into slavery in Egypt. The wife of Joseph's master tried to seduce him. As a result of him not complying he ended up in prison. Circumstances then made him the king of Egypt's chief minister. In this position of authority he invited people to worship God alone.

Reading and reflecting on the Quranic verses surrounding this story can be beneficial to anyone struggling to find a way out of their own problems.

JOSEPH'S FATHER TELLS HIM TO GUARD HIS DREAM
"O my father! Verily, I saw (in a dream) eleven stars and the sun and the moon, I saw them prostrating themselves to me." "O my son! Relate not your vision to your brothers, lest they arrange a plot against you. Verily! Satan is to man an open enemy! Thus will your Lord choose you and teach you the interpretation of dreams (and other things) and perfect His Favor on you and on the offspring of Jacob, as He perfected it on your fathers, Abraham, and Isaac aforetime! Verily! your Lord is All-Knowing, All-Wise." (Quran 12:4-6)

HIS BROTHERS THINK OF KILLING HIM
"Truly, Joseph and his brother (Benjamin) are loved more by our father than we, but we are a strong group. Really our father is in plain error. Kill Joseph or cast him out to some other land, so that the favor of your father may be given to you alone, and after that you will be righteous folk (by intending repentance before committing the sin)." One from among them said: "Kill not Joseph, but if you must do something, throw him down to the bottom of a well, he will be picked up by some caravan of travelers." (Quran 12:8-10)

JOSEPH FOUND BY A CARAVAN OF TRAVELLERS
"And there came a caravan of travellers; they sent their water drawer, and he let down his bucket into the well. He said: "What good news! Here is a boy." So they hid him as merchandise (a slave). And God was the All Knower of what they did. They sold him for a low price, for a few silver coins. They were of those who regarded him insignificant. He (the man) from Egypt who bought him said to his wife: "Make his stay comfortable, maybe he will profit us or we shall adopt him as

a son." Thus did We establish Joseph in the land, that We might teach him the interpretation of events. (Quran 12:19-21)

HIS MASTER'S WIFE TRIES TO SEDUCE JOSEPH
"And she, in whose house he was, sought to seduce him (to do an evil act), she closed the doors and said: "come on, O you." He said: "I seek refuge in God (or God forbid)! Truly he (your husband) is my master! He made my stay agreeable! (So I will never betray him). Verily, the evildoers will never be successful." Indeed she did desire him and he would have inclined to her desire had he not seen the evidence of his Lord: thus (did we order) that We might turn away from him (all) evil and indecent deeds: for he was one of Our chosen servants. (Quran 12:23-24)

HIS MASTER'S WIFE ACCUSES JOSEPH
"It was she that sought to seduce me," and a witness of her household bore witness saying: "If it be that his shirt is torn from the front, then her tale is true, and he is a liar! but if it be that his shirt is torn from the back, then she has told a lie and he is speaking the truth!" So when he (the husband) saw his (Joseph's) shirt was torn at the back; (her husband) said: "Surely, it is a plot of you women! certainly mighty is your plot! O Joseph! turn away from this! (O woman)! ask forgiveness for your sin. Verily, you were of the sinful."(Quran 12:26-29).

JOSEPH ASKS TO BE SENT TO PRISON TO PROTECT HIS CHASITY
He said: "O my Lord! Prison is more to my liking than that to which they invite me. Unless You turn away their plot from me, I will feel inclined towards them and be one of those who commit sin and deserve blame or those who do deeds of the ignorant." So his Lord answered his invocation and turned away from him their plot. Verily he is the All Hearer, the All Knower." (Quran 12:31-34)

JOSEPH INTERPRETS DREAMS
"And there entered with him two young men in the prison. One of them said: "Verily, I saw myself (in a dream) pressing wine." The other said: "Verily, I saw myself (in a dream) carrying bread on my head and birds were eating thereof." They said: Inform us of the interpretation of this. Verily, we think you are one of those doers of good." He said: "No food will come to you (in wakefulness or in dream) as your provision but I will inform (in wakefulness) its interpretation before it (the food) comes. This is of that which my Lord has taught me. Verily, I have abandoned the religion of a people that believe not in God and are disbelievers in the Hereafter. And I have followed the religion of my fathers, - Abraham, Isaac, and Jacob and never could we attribute any partners whatsoever to God. This is from the Grace of God to us and to mankind, but most men think not (i.e. they neither believe in God nor worship Him). "O two companions of the

prison! Are many different lords (gods) better or God, the One, the Irresistible? You do not worship besides Him but only names which you have named (forged), you and your fathers, for which God has sent down no authority. The command (or the judgment) is for none but God. He has commanded (His Monotheism), that is the true, straight religion, but most men know not. "O two companions of the prison! As for one of you, he (as a servant) will pour out wine for his lord (King or master) to drink; and as for the other, he will be crucified and birds will eat from his head. Thus is the case concerning which you both did inquire." And he said to the one whom he knew to be saved: "Mention me to your lord (your King, so to get me out of the prison)." But Satan made him forget to mention it to his lord. So Joseph stayed in prison a few more years. (Quran 12:36-42).

THE KING HAS A DREAM AND JOSEPH WAS SUMMONED

Almighty God said: And the king said: "Bring him to me." But, when the messenger came to him Joseph said: "Return to your lord, and ask him, 'what happened to the women who cut their hands? Surely, my Lord (God) is Well Aware of their plot." (The king) said (to the women): "What was your affair when you did seek to seduce Joseph?" The women said: "God forbid! No evil know we against him!" The wife of Al Aziz said: "Now the truth is manifest to all, it was I who sought to seduce him and he is surely one of the truthful." (Then Joseph said: "I asked for this inquiry) in order that he (Al-Aziz) may know that I betrayed him not in secret. And, verily! God guides not the plot of the betrayers. And I free myself (from the blame). Verily, the human self is inclined to evil, except when my Lord bestows His Mercy (upon whom He wills). Verily, my Lord is Oft-Forgiving, most Merciful." (Quran 12:50-53).

Joseph was proved innocent of sexual seduction and became the minister of finance for Egypt. In his high position he invited others to believe in God alone. He was later reunited with his brothers and his father Prophet Jacob (peace be upon him).

MOSES / MUSA
(peace be upon him)

It may surprise you to know that much of Prophet Moses's (peace be upon him) life is also reported in the Quran. Muslims accept him as one of the mighty messengers of God. Below are some excerpts from the Quran.

GOD SPOKE TO MOSES
"Of some messengers We have already told you the story; of others We have not; - and to Moses God spoke direct." (Quran 4:164)

HIS CALL TO PROPHETHOOD
"Now when Moses had fulfilled the term, and was travelling with his family, he perceived a fire in the direction of Mount Tur. He said to his family: 'Remain here; I perceive a fire; I hope to bring you from there some information, or a burning firebrand, that you may warm yourselves.' But he came to the (Fire), he was called from the right bank of the valley, from a tree in hallowed ground: 'O Moses! Verily I am God, the Lord of the Worlds... Now throw your rod!' But when he saw it moving (of its own accord) as if it had been a snake, he turned back in retreat, and retraced his steps: 'O Moses!' (It was said), 'Draw near, and fear not: for you are of those who are secure. Thrust your hand into your bosom, and it will come forth white without stain (or harm), and draw your hand close to your side (to guard) against fear. Those are the two credentials from your Lord to Pharaoh and his Chiefs: for truly they are a people rebellious and wicked.' " (Quran 28:29-32)

GOD STRENGTHENS MOSES WITH AARON
"He said: 'We will certainly strengthen your arm through your brother, and invest you both with authority, so they shall not be able to touch you: with Our Signs shall you triumph, you two as well as those who follow you.' " (Quran 28:35)

SENT TO PHARAOH WITH AARON
"Go, you and your brother, with My signs, and slacken not, either of you, in keeping Me in remembrance. Go both of you, to Pharaoh, for he has indeed transgressed all bounds; But speak to him mildly; perchance he may take warning or fear (God)."(Quran 20:42-44)

" 'So go you both to him, and say, 'Verily we are Messengers sent by your Lord: send forth, therefore, the children of Israel with us, and afflict them not: with a Sign, indeed, have we come from your Lord! And Peace to all who follow guidance!' " (Quran 20:47)

PHARAOH AND HIS ARMY DROWNS

"We sent an inspiration to Moses: 'Travel by night with My servants and strike a dry path for them through the sea, without fear of being overtaken (by Pharaoh) and without (any other) fear.' Then Pharaoh pursued them with his forces, but the waters completely overwhelmed them and covered them. Pharaoh led his people astray instead of leading them aright." (Quran 20:77-79)

DAVID/DAWUD
(peace be upon him)

David was a soldier in King Saul's army. He rose to fame when he volunteered to take on Goliath. Using a sling he was able to kill Goliath by striking him on the head. Saul rewarded David with marriage to his daughter.

DAVID CHOSEN AS A PROPHET AND GIVEN THE PSALMS

"Verily, We made the mountains to glorify Our Praises with him (David) at eventide and at break of day, and (so did) the birds assembled: all with him (David) did turn (to God). We made his kingdom strong and gave him wisdom and sound judgment in speech and decision. (Quran 38:18-20)

Creatures such as the plants, birds, beasts, and even the mountains responded to his voice glorifying God. God had chosen David to be a prophet and revealed the Psalms to him. As He the Almighty said: "And to David We gave the Psalms." (Quran 17:55).

With time Saul was killed in battle, and David becomes king.

DAVID BECOMES KING

"So they routed them by God's Leave and David killed Goliath, and God gave him (David) the kingdom (after the death of Saul and Samuel) and wisdom, and taught him of that which He willed. And if God did not check one set of people by means of another, the earth would indeed be full of mischief. But God is full of Bounty to the worlds. (Quran 2:251).

Prophet David was known as a just and righteous ruler. He left behind a son Solomon, who also was chosen by God to be a prophet.

SOLOMON/SULAIMAN
(peace be upon him)

SOLOMON INHERITS DAVID'S PROPHETHOOD

"And indeed We gave knowledge to David and Solomon, and they both said: "All praises and thanks be to God, Who has preferred us above many of His believing slaves!" And Solomon inherited (the knowledge of) David. He said: "O mankind! We have been taught the language of birds, and on us has been bestowed all things. This, verily, is an evident grace (from God)." And there were gathered before Solomon his hosts of jinns and men, and birds, and they were all set in battle order (marching forwards). (Quran 27:15-17).

SHOWERED WITH GIFTS FROM GOD

"And to David We gave Solomon. How excellent a slave! Verily, he was ever oft returning in repentance (to Us)! When there were displayed before him, in the afternoon, well-trained horses of the highest breed, he said: "Alas! I did love the good (these horses) instead of remembering my Lord (in my 'Asr prayer)" till the time was over, and the sun had hidden in the veil of the night. Then he said: "Bring them (horses) back to me." Then he began to pass his hand over their legs and their necks (till the end of the display). And indeed We did try Solomon and We placed on his throne a devil, (so he lost his kingdom for a while) but he did return (to his throne and kingdom by the Grace of God and he did return) to God with obedience and in repentance. He said: "My Lord! Forgive me, and bestow upon me a kingdom such as shall not belong to any other after me. Verily, You are the Bestower." So, We subjected to him the wind, it blew gently to his order whithersoever he willed, and also the devils from the jinns including every kind of builder and diver, and also other bound in fetters. (Saying of God to Solomon): "This is Our gift, so spend you or withhold, no account will be asked." And verily, he enjoyed a near access to Us, and a final return Paradise. (Quran 38:30-40).

SOLOMON SENDS A LETTER TO THE QUEEN OF SHEBA

"He inspected the birds, and said: "What is the matter that I see not a hoopoe? Or is he among the absentees? I will surely punish him with a severe torment, or slaughter him, unless he brings me a clear reason." But the hoopoe stayed not long, he came up and said: "I have grasped (the knowledge of a thing) which you have not grasped and I have come to you from Sheba with true news. I found a woman ruling over them, and she has been given all things that could be possessed by any ruler of the earth, and she has a great throne. I found her and her people worshipping the sun instead of God, and Satan has made their deeds fair seeming to them, and has barred them from God's Way, so they have no guidance." (Quran 27: 20-24)

(Solomon) said: "We shall see whether you speak the truth or you are one of the liars. Go with this letter of mine, and deliver it to them, then draw back from them, and see what answer they return." She said: "O chiefs! Verily! Here is a delivered to me a noble letter. Verily! It is from Solomon and verily! It (reads): 'In the Name of God, the Most Beneficent, the Most Merciful; Be you not exalted against me, but come to me as Muslims (true believers who submit to God with full submission)." (Quran 27: 27-31)

THE QUEEN OF SHEBA AND SOLOMAN MEETS
She said: "O chiefs! Advise me in this case of mine. I decide no case till you are present with me." They said: "We have great strength, and great ability for war, but it is for you to command; so think over what you will command." She said: "Verily! Kings, when they enter a town (country), they despoil it, and make the most honorable amongst its people low. And thus they do. But verily! I am going to send him a present, and see with what answer the messengers return." So when (the messengers with the present) came to Solomon, he said: "Will you help me in wealth? What God has given me is better than that which He has given you! Nay, you rejoice in your gift!" (Then Solomon said to the chief of her messengers who brought the present): "Go back to them. We verily shall come to them with hosts that they cannot resist, and we shall drive them out from there is disgrace, and they will be abased." He said: "O chiefs! Which of you can bring me her throne before they come to me surrendering themselves in obedience?" And a strong from the jinns said: "I will bring it to you before you rise from your place (council). And verily, I am indeed strong, and trustworthy for such work." One with whom was knowledge of the Scripture said: "I will bring it to you within the twinkling of an eye!" then when Solomon saw it placed before him, he said: "This is by the Grace of my Lord, to test me whether I am grateful or ungrateful! And whoever is grateful, truly, his gratitude is for the good of his ownself, and whoever is ungrateful, he is ungrateful only for the loss of his ownself. Certainly! My Lord is Rich (Free of all wants), Bountiful!" (Quran 27: 32-40)

He said: "Disguise her throne for her that we may see whether she will be guided (to recognize her throne), or she will be one of those not guided." So when she came, it was said to her: "Is your throne like this?" She said: "It is as though it was the very same." And Solomon said: "Knowledge was bestowed on us before her, and we were submitted to God (in Islam as Muslims before her)." And that which she used to worship besides God has prevented her from Islam, for she was of a disbelieving people. (Quran 27: 41-43)

THE QUEEN OF SHEBA BECOMES A MUSLIM

It was said to her: "Enter the lofty Palace", but when she saw it, she thought it was a pool, and she tucked up her clothes, uncovering her legs. Solomon said: "Verily, it is a palace paved smooth with slab of glass." She said: "My Lord! Verily, I have wronged myself, and I submit (in Islam), with Solomon, to God, the Lord of the Worlds." (Quran 27: 44)

The queen of Sheba (Bilqis) gave up sun worshipping and became a Muslim. Her people followed in her footsteps.

JESUS / ISA
(peace be upon him)

Muslims are required to believe in Jesus (peace be upon him). Muslims believe he is a prophet of God. Muslims also believe in the virgin birth of Jesus (peace by upon him). The entire incident is narrated in a chapter of the Quran titled Maryam (Mary). Below are portions of the chapter describing the virgin birth of Jesus (peace be upon him) as well as other portions of the Quran detailing other aspects of his life.

VIRGIN BIRTH

"Relate in the Book (the story of) Mary, when she withdrew from her family to a place in the East. She placed a screen (to screen herself) from them: then We sent to her Our angel, and he appeared before her as a man in all respects. She said: 'I seek refuge from you to (God) Most Gracious: (come not near) if you do fear God.' He said: 'Nay, I am only a messenger from your Lord (to announce) to you the gift of a pure son.' She said: 'How shall I have a son, seeing that no man has touched me, and I am not unchaste?' He said: 'So (it will be): Your Lord said: 'That is easy for Me: and (We wish) to appoint him as a Sign unto men and a mercy from Us': it is a matter (so) decreed.' " (Quran 19:16-21)

JESUS WAS NOT THE SON OF GOD

"Christ the son of Mary was no more than a Messenger; many were the Messengers that passed away before him. His mother was a woman of truth. They both had to eat their (daily) food. See how God does make His Signs clear to them; yet see in what ways they are deluded away from the truth!" (Quran 5:75)

"The similitude of Jesus before God is as that of Adam, he created him from dust, then said to him: 'Be': and he was." (Quran 3:59)

PERFORMED MIRACLES

"Behold! The Disciples said: 'O Jesus the son of Mary! Can your Lord send down to us a Table set (with viands) from heaven?' Said Jesus: 'Fear God, if you have faith' They said: 'We only wish to eat thereof and satisfy our hearts, and to know that you have indeed told us the truth; and that we ourselves may be witnesses to the miracle.' Said Jesus the son of Mary: 'O God our Lord! Send us from heaven a table set (with viands), that there may be for us -for the first and the last of us - a solemn festival and a Sign from You; and provide for our sustenance, for You are the best Sustainer (of our needs).' God said: 'I will send it down unto you: but if any of you after that resists faith, I will punish him with chastisement such as I have not inflicted on any one among all the peoples.' " (Quran 5:112-115)

FORETOLD THE COMING OF MUHAMMAD

"And remember, Jesus, the son of Mary, said: 'O children of Israel! I am the Messenger of God (sent) to you, confirming the Torah (which came) before me, and giving glad tidings of a Messenger to come after me, whose name shall be **Ahmad**. But when he came to them with Clear Signs, they said: 'This is evident sorcery!' '" (Quran 61:6)

WAS NOT KILLED

"That they said (in boast): 'We killed Christ Jesus the son of Mary, the Messenger of God' but they killed him not, nor crucified him. Only a likeness of that was shown to them. And those who differ therein are full of doubts, with no (certain) knowledge. But only conjecture to follow, for of a surety they killed him not. Nay, God raised him up unto Himself; and God is Exalted in Power, Wise." (Quran 4:157-158)

MUHAMMAD
(peace be upon him)

Muslims consider Muhammad (peace be upon him) to be God's last known prophet and Messenger to mankind.

He was born in Arabia in the year 570 of the Christian era. He was called to prophethood at the age of 40 and died at the age of 63. The Quran, which we have referred to throughout this book, was revealed to him in small amounts over 23 years.

In this short span of 23 years he was able to change the whole of the Arabian Peninsula from idol-worship and paganism to the worship of God; from moral decay to moral excellence; from tribal wars to solidarity and purpose; from the exploitation of women and killing of female babies to respect for females.

The Encyclopedia Britannica calls him "the most successful of all religious personalities of the world." Others had this to say:

"My choice of Muhammad to lead the list of the world's most influential persons may surprise some readers and may be questioned by others, but he was the only man in history who was supremely successful on both the religious and secular levels." (From: *The 100 - A Ranking of the Most Influential Persons in History* by Michael H. Hart.)

"People like Pasteur and Salk are leaders in the first sense. People like Ghandi and Confucius, on one hand, and Alexander, Caesar and Hitler on the other, are leaders in the second and perhaps the third sense. Jesus and Buddha belong in the third category alone. Perhaps the greatest leader of all times was Mohammed, who combined all three functions. To a lesser degree Moses did the same." (Professor Jules Masserman)

"Philosopher, Orator, Apostle, Legislator, Warrior, Conqueror of ideas, Restorer of rational beliefs, of a cult without images; the founder of twenty-terrestrial empires and of one spiritual empire, that is Muhammad. As regards all standards by which human greatness may be measured, we may well ask, is there any man greater than he?" (From: *Historie de la Turquie* by Alphonse de LaMartine).

Today he is followed by over one billion Muslims worldwide. Below are some verses from the Quran relating to Prophet Muhammad (peace be upon him).

WAS A HUMAN BEING

"Say: 'I am but a man like yourselves, (but) the inspiration has come to me, that your God is one God: whoever expects to meet his Lord, let him work righteousness, and, in the worship of his Lord, admit no one as partner.' " (Quran 18:110)

ANGEL GABRIEL BROUGHT REVELATION TO HIM

The very same angel Gabriel, that brought revelation to the earlier prophets, also brought revelation to Prophet Muhammad (peace be upon him). The Quran tells us:

"Verily this (the Quran) is a Revelation from the Lord of the Worlds: With it came down the truthful spirit to your heart that you may admonish. In the perspicuous Arabic tongue." (Quran 26:192-195)

INVITED PEOPLE TO WORSHIP THE ONE AND ONLY GOD

Say, [O Muhammad], "I am only a warner, and there is not any deity except God , the One, the Prevailing. (38:65)

MESSENGER TO ALL MANKIND

"We have not sent you but as a (Messenger) to all mankind, giving them glad tidings, and warning them (against sin), but most men know not." (Quran 34:28)

SEAL TO PROPHETHOOD

"Muhammad is not the father of any of your men, but (he is) the Messenger of God, and the Seal of the Prophets, and God has full knowledge of all things." (Quran 33:40)

In simple terms, there are no more Prophets of God to come, and his final revelation (the Quran) is with mankind.

SUMMARY

When Muslims teach their children the stories of the lives of the prophets, they not only teach about the life of Prophet Muhammad (peace be upon him, who Muslims believe was the last prophet from God), but also about:

(a)   The miraculous birth of Jesus (peace be upon him), as well as the fact that he was able to perform miracles by God's permission. *Christian*

(b)   The story of Moses (peace be upon him), his upbringing and his eventual confrontation with Pharaoh's oppression. *Jewish Christian*

(c)   Abraham's (peace be upon him) search for God. His destruction of the idols of his people and God's cooling of the fire when his people tried to burn him for his act of rebellion. *Jewish Christian*

(d)   The lives of Noah, Joseph, Solomon, Jonah, and other prophets (peace be upon them) are also taught.

All these prophets' stories are in the Quran, God's final revelation to mankind.

One thing that struck me as I was researching this book is that the people at the times of various Prophets suffered specific moral challenges. Examples: the people of Adam – jealousy, Noah – disbelief, Abraham – idol worship and Lot – homosexuality.

Today, the world is a global village. Collectively, we suffer from all of the above, and more. How this will all play out only time will tell. In the meantime, do all you can to protect yourself and those that you love.

God Bless!

TRANSLATIONS OF THE QURAN

The Quran was revealed to Prophet Muhammad (peace be upon him) in the Arabic language. For those wanting to read the Quran in English, and to find out more about the twenty-five prophets of Islam, the following are recommended translations:

1. The Noble Quran by Muhammad Al-Hilali and Muhammad Muhsin Khan.

2. The Holy Quran by Yusuf Ali.

3. The Message of the Quran by Muhammad Asad.

4. The Glorious Quran by Marmaduke Pickthall.

5. The Holy Qu'ran in Today's English by Yahiya Emerick.

AN INVITATION

Irfan Alli

On completing an earlier eBook titled _101 Selected Quotes on Making a Difference_ I wondered what I could do to help make the world a better place and more specifically to help people in their day to day struggles for a better life. If only I knew someone who was struggling or who needed money for a business venture to make life better for his family, who wasn't just looking for a hand out but a hand up...so I started poking around the internet to see what I could find.

I did not want to simply give money to a charity and have them find people who needed help. I wanted to pick and choose those people myself. I did not want to simply give the money away but wanted it to be an interest free loan. Money that gets paid back and can then be used to help others if I choose. I found _Kiva._

I joined _Kiva_ and formed a team called _Helping Hands International_ to encourage readers like you as well as friends and relatives to help improve the lives of others.

If you would like to make a difference I invite you to join _Kiva_ and my team on _Kiva_ called _Helping Hands International._

ABOUT KIVA

Kiva is a non-denominational international organization that partners with locals in 83 different countries all over the world and monitors the funds that are micro financed out to deserving people/projects, and the best thing is YOU decide who is deserving and how much you want to lend!

Its members lend a minimum of $25.00 at a time to a borrower of choice. The money you give is not a grant. It is a LOAN. And *Kiva* has a 98.95% repayment rate of all loans. That means the people who get the funds, repay the loan and it eventually goes back into YOUR pot to help others!

When you lend $25.00 through *Kiva, Kiva* forwards the money at a zero interest rate to a local microfinance institution that is in contact with the person you want to lend money to. The microfinance institution earmarks the money to the specific person you chose. When the client repays, the money comes back to *Kiva*, then to your account, ready to be loaned again to someone of your choosing.

The most impressive part of *Kiva* is that it's lent over half a BILLION dollars to poor people all over the world using money coming from people like you and me. *Kiva* brings people's lives to our computers and gives us an opportunity to make a difference!!!

It's like you can see the struggling farmer, and from the goodness of your heart, and the hearts of countless others, you can reach out and give $25 at a time!

And everyone I know can afford to give $25 at a time! We spend that on coffee every month! It's chump change!

You can watch videos on how *Kiva* works on YouTube.

ABOUT HELPING HANDS INTERNATIONAL

Helping Hands International is a team I initiated on *Kiva* to get relatives, friends and readers like you to join hands together to make a difference. I believe that among the best actions we can do is "gladden the hearts of other human beings, feed the hungry, help the afflicted, lighten the sorrow of the sorrowful and remove the sufferings of the injured." My personal commitment is to help at least one thousand people. I hope I live long enough to get there! You can see our *Kiva* loans to date at *Helping Hands International*.

Many of the teams on *Kiva* are named after a person, a place, a religion, an orientation, a country or a philosophy. *Helping Hands International* invites anyone living anywhere in the world to come together to help people anywhere in the world despite color, language or nationality. As a result the name *Helping Hands International*. No ideological or religious connection, just filling practical needs!

First join *Kiva* and then join team *Helping Hands International*.

Hope to see you on board!

Irfan Alli

irfanalli@irfanalli.com

OTHER EBOOKS BY THE AUTHOR

All eBooks are available on Amazon, Kobo, Apple (iTunes), Barnes and Noble, Ingram Digital, ebookit.com, Baker and Taylor, Google and many others. They are available in various delivery formats. Below is a listing of current titles:

SPOUSE TRAP - Over 200 Questions to Ask Before Saying "I do"

WHAT HAPPENS AFTER WE DIE?

ISLAM AND MUSLIMS – A Collection of Questions and Answers

WHAT ARE ANGELS?

101 SELECTED SAYINGS OF PROPHET MUHAMMAD (peace be upon him)

ENLIGHTENMENT FROM THE QURAN – God's Last Revelation to Mankind

HOW TO GET THE MOST OUT OF SCHOOL – A Practical Guide for Students and Parents

201 MOTIVATIONAL QUOTES FROM AROUND THE WORLD

101 SELECTED SAYINGS OF MAHATMA GANDHI

CONDOMINIUMS AND TOWNHOUSES – What You Need to Know Before and After Buying

101 SELECTED SAYINGS OF BUDDHA

FAMILY MAKEOVERS

SHORTCUTS TO HEAVEN

CONTACT: Irfan Alli can be reached at irfanalli@irfanalli.com

A PERSONAL MESSAGE FROM THE AUTHOR

Thank you for purchasing this book. I hope it was beneficial.

In return, please be generous and take the time to write a review. It doesn't have to be glowing, just genuine and fair. To do so please go to www.amazon.com, search the title of the book and post your review.

Thanks for doing so!

Irfan Alli

Printed in Great Britain
by Amazon